If You Don't Mind

Leizly Munoz

BookLeaf
Publishing

India | USA | UK

If You Don't Mind © 2024 Leizly Munoz

All rights reserved.

No part of this publication may be reproduced, stored in a retrieval system, or transmitted, in any form or by any means, electronic, mechanical, photocopying, recording or otherwise, without the prior written permission of the presenters.

Leizly Munoz asserts the moral right to be identified as author of this work.

Presentation by *BookLeaf Publishing*

Web: www.bookleafpub.com

E-mail: info@bookleafpub.com

ISBN: 9789363301023

First edition 2024

ACKNOWLEDGEMENT

To those whom I've shared laughter with until tears flowed.

Thank you.

You

I delve in your touch and sounds,
Finding meaning by your side.
Your laughter I crave and hound,
In your skin I want to hide.

I love to be loved,
I love to love you, too.
I hate that you I'd never get sick of,
I hate how I could never really hate you.

Road's Rage

As I drive on your hot, dry, rocky skin,
My tires, you make paper thin.

The agonizing hum you make when we collide,
But we all want to go home, the sound so
amplified.

I'm sorry for taking your solitary beauty away,
now covered in potholes and blemishes, even on
the highway.

Through my selfish need to eat and sleep,
we all sit on your surface and hear you weep.

It's the traffic that gets to me the most,
our daily destruction is your lethal dose.

Comfort in Severance

My door swings open, and I hide,
I hear heavy movements, side to side.
He breaks in every day at the same time,
With a key, I can hear the chime.

I consider it my fault,
I have a key to lock the house like a vault.
I slowly approach, the atmosphere thick,
What if he's armed? All I can do is kick.

There's a stranger in my house,
I hear him in the kitchen, rummaging like a
mouse.
I hold my breath, my heart starts to race,
Can't believe there's someone in my space.

Footsteps grow louder, and towards I creep,
I inch forward, afraid to make a peep.
The air is tense, can't believe my eyes,
I finally confront the intruder, it's my partner to
my surprise.

Thursday

Thursday, the second day from the weekend,
Where the work week begins to descend,
And holding on to Friday is bearable again.

The day that feels like the color purple.
Mixes of courageous red and gloomy blues
begin to circle.
Surrounding your mind, overlooking Friday
evening like a portal.

It's almost done; It's almost over.
It's 4:26 p.m.; my mind's a rover.
And the clock, my eye's secret lover.

The Tragedy to Hopeful Love

Your mouth hisses words that your actions could
never catch,
With every race, my heart gains another scratch.
Empty promises seem to last forever,
Always broken, always the lesser.

Absence isn't reassurance,
An often recurrence,
Love-bombing after you see my deflection,
We never seem to head in the right direction.
Together at least,
Each other we should release.

The ache and misery need to rest,
Perhaps letting go is a test we must digest.
But not right now,
I'll continue to allow,
One day I might wake up to find you're
consistent,
That what you allege and your efforts are finally
coexistent.

The version that I see of you,
I have so much hope you'll turn into,

Perhaps that's where I went wrong and
misconstrued,
But that's the version of you I met in our
prelude.

My Solace

My friend brings me laughter, a great elation,
Mending a heart she didn't break, a great
salvation.
Unaware she's even aiding, she enjoys my
company,
From shopping sprees to mending a broken
heart,
An ensemble, She's next to me unreluctantly.

Inseparable, like gum tangled in hair,
She's my best friend, together we plan to explore
everywhere.
Watching her blossom, while I mature too,
Together we find comfort in the familiar and the
new.

In our pilgrimage through life, we seek each
other for advice,
To share updates, to laugh, and to cry,
I know my friend is genuine,
And replacing her, I could never try.

Dancing Around the Void

With no one to break my fall,
And having to feel it all.
The pain of losing another half I have to feel,
A pain that's common, hard to believe it's real.

A life-altering occurrence I attempted to
postpone,
From sharing a space and clothes to eating
alone.
Never realizing the comfort physical warmth
brings,
Or how loud the silence echoes and clings.

Like a word that's on the tip of my tongue,
Knowing what needs to be done but never sung,
Memories that have been plagued,
A nick to my heart like a sharp blade.

To see you no longer feels the same,
But to tell you, I'll be the one you blame.
I know you feel how I feel too,
But you'll always mask it with an "I love you."

The Moon's Secret

Gazing at the night sky, the moonlight, a
whisper, barely visible,
Yet it's still there, a twinkle in my eye, light still
transmissible.
Tomorrow, it will camouflage with the shadows,
Though out of sight, It will float in the
darkness's shallows.

Two weeks from now, it will be halfway full,
I adore the moon's nightly pull
Emerging from the suede darkness,
A bit more, a bit less, each night.
Three weeks from now, it will glisten,
Happy to illuminate and live its life in sight.

Then it will slowly tuck itself to bed.
The moon knows something we don't, its not
our friend.
Nurturing itself, knowing when to gleam or stay
hidden.
Nothing I do can affect its behavior, it's
unbidden.

I stand in awe at the labor it endures,
Emerging like a butterfly from a cocoon.

Millions see, then the world it tours,
The waves cry for the moon.

But the moon will not cry back,
For it knows itself, opacity it will never lack.
No matter how many clouds attack,
I might not see it tomorrow, but I know it's
between the cracks.

The moon, confident in its existence, needing to
prove nothing.
It'll emerge tomorrow, the moon is very cunning.

Bubble

The film between being alive and living,
The separation from experiences is unforgiving,
Like a viewer to your own life, never directing.

Only grasping the moments they become
memories,
Realizing your mind and heart might be
accessories,
Decorations to the vessel of daily
documentaries.

A stranger in my own home is a haunting
experience,
Like a body that doesn't agree with coexistence,
with the lack of detail being my evidence.

Life, a transparent film I board,
And no clue where we're going towards,
Living on autopilot, but no life explored.

Life is to see, to hurt, and to cry,
To feel, to love, and to try,
Not to free-fall like a bubble in the sky.

Essence of Solitude

Some days, I'm engulfed by life,
Some days, it's like butter on a hot knife.
My own space, like my own time,
I can do whatever, I'm in my prime.

Loneliness sounds scarier than it is,
But company is a luxury, and you got used to
his.
No one to cater to, no one to baby,
A habit hard to heal, necessary but the process is
shaky

With no one's fears to stop me,
Everything I do is up to me.
I can stare at the sky for hours, or enjoy long
showers,
With no one to boss me, no one to carry.

It's all about me tonight and maybe tomorrow,
and my fear to be alone,
I have to put to rest, bury, and let go.
My subsistence is the the only thing I own.

998 Lifeline Pl.

Walking in the darkness, like trying to find a
light,
Unfamiliar with the switch, the shadows give me
fright.
What's lurking in the shadows? I'm scared
someone might grab me,
My chest is filling up with cement, my lungs a
black sea.

Though I can't see, somehow I see even less,
Cement submerges my lungs, aiming for my
head next.
Floor like quicksand, I sink the more I provoke,
The thought of moving, breath quickens, my
body starts to choke.

Where are the lights? Why am I here?
Holding my breath, swallowed by fear.
The earth craves the suspense my mind creates,
Quicksand's slow demo, my personal hell's
gates.

Quicksand is not so quick, it puts on a show and
a song,

A neuronic visualization of everything that can
go wrong.
The silence pounds like concert's bass,
My mouth fills with sand, words erased.

Suspended in my mind, till earth decides,
To spit me back up, then the darkness hides.
For now, holding my breath is all I can do,
As I submerge deeper, anxiety begins its brew.

Mindful Freedom

I'm off again, I feel free, liberated, it slipped my
mind.
Was I upset? Life is great and kind.
The urge to run outside, feel the breeze through
my hair,
A transient joy, but I don't care.

Guilt whispers, I know it's temporary,
A self-induced happiness, a momentary
sanctuary.
It's taking time for it all to make sense,
But I'll savor this lightness, this pretense.

Anything that happens is tomorrow's concern,
For now, I'll let the weightlessness return.

Absence in Wholeness

Falling out of love feels like a puzzle you can't
complete,
Promised 50 pieces,
But only got 43.
"Maybe I lost one between the cushions," you
find one more piece.

44, yet still missing a few.
You're confused, the box brand-new,
Scanning the floor for any other clue.
Finding none, and you know what you must do.

One last glance at your time-consuming
masterpiece,
A pastime that once brought you peace.
Now, you're noticing every bend, every crease.
Forcing the completion to cease.

The fragments you begin to break apart,
analyzing their tattooed design.
You think about how every slice, another one
has to align,
Remembering how close you were, you
dismantle them line by line.
From love to hate, the feelings now benign.

Finally done, you tuck the box away,
Debating discarding it or if it should stay.
Any other puzzle, you'll hold the memory and delay,
You'll always remember how it felt, to be disappointed and hurt today.

Bittersweet Taste of Time

One day the toothpaste no longer burned,
Another day and candy we no longer yearned,
Wanting to grow up then, but now we learned,
That in a heartbeat we'd like return.

Only dealing with scrapped knees and scratched
DVDs,
Today we pay extraneous bills and hella fees,
Not knowing then that life was a cool breeze,
Hearing the birds chirp, and living carefree.

Now, toothpaste is tasteless and life is muted,
Desserts and sweets are putrid,
At least that's what social media has polluted,
But these are the good times, I have now
concluded.

Good Morning

Hours and hours have gone by.
And it appears the sun has said goodbye.

The moon is bright, but not as illuminating as
the sun.
Bringing an unknown darkness I can no longer
outrun.

Only being able to move because the moon
shines its light,
Creating a path I can only see so far into the
night.

Wandering with no plan has been just as cold.
I forgot I was looking for tomorrow's gold.

Now, the sun has risen, reaching a new height,
But it's a new sun, casting a different light.

The rays shine, my skin its warmth gently bites,
but this time around, it feels so right.

The blankets of the night are out of sight.
Will this sun bring a darkness of its own?
It could. It might.

1 New Message

Between messages, I can't seem to catch you at
the right time.
Always hours away, I begin to wonder if you
were ever mine.
The ache of missing you is torture by design,

My longing to converse feels like a crime.
One new message, your name on my screen is so
divine,
"I miss you too," my heart and mind begin to
realign.

Together now, our time finally intertwined.
No matter the distance, a path we will always
find.

Digital Delirium

Glued to the screen, your eyes begin to water
and burn,
A sting that swells and your eyes want to turn.
But you're in the zone and your eyes are on a
quest,
Trying to not lose the 8-hour staring contest.

Hours go by and you begin to see through the
screen,
Observing the individual pixels, the red, the
blue, and the green.
Consuming minuscule lights, for hours a day,
It's hard to believe they create a display.

Okay, enough. You're losing focus.
We can't let any thoughts provoke us,
But the letters and numbers begin to look
foreign,
And you know you got to look away from the
black and white distortion.

Sixteen

Young love could never compare,
To what later relationships have prepared.

A love so undeveloped, a love so sweet,
A secret from our parents we keep.

Sixteen and living life free,
With a guy being my only worry.

Late-night park meet-ups and 2 a.m. walks,
December winds and late-night talks.

Our noses frosty cold and numb,
Never knowing what love could become.

Lack of communication was fine,
A love much easier, a simple design.

So long ago now, collecting dust,
A memory now that ended with distrust.

A soreness that was much easier to endure,
That's the beauty of puppy love, feelings needed
to mature.

Lessons learned and innocence gone,
The simplicity has withdrawn.

Like tumbleweeds, we danced with the wind,
Now blown apart, but we moved on and we still
lived.

Dusk to Dawn

Sometimes, I wake up tired, just as others often
do,
Desire to cling to my sheets, their company feels
so true.
Now I'm racing against time, my hair refusing to
obey,
Just like everyone else, my morning's a cliché.

A craving that claws, yearning for sleep's retreat,
Maybe everyone knows this feeling, a cycle
that's been on repeat.
Tripping over my own feet, stumbling on my
tongue,
Isn't this common? But the day is still young.

A hazy fog shields my eyes, sleep might claim
this win,
Everyone goes through this, right? And my head
begins to spin.
Tripping over my own feet again, wanting to fall
and longing for my bed,
Perhaps it's not normal, hanging by a thread.

The Moon's SecretWhatever, It's Just an Honest Confession, but Can I Call You?

Where East and West meet in the middle,
Your love is so strong,
I feel it, just a little,
Someone like you I couldn't prolong, you're
what I've always wanted all along.

You talk about my hair and how you like it,
You know deepest seas, and you still seek more
to adore,
My feelings are stuck in my throat, I'll admit.
But I love the feeling, with each emotion you
pour.

Lost in thought, are we doing this?
You feel what I feel too?
Feeling the lightning strike inside and turn to
bliss.
Raw and sweet like honey, a sensation worth the
renew.

It's frightening yet exhilarating,

Like bungee jumping from a bridge,
But with you, it's more facilitating.
If this is love, then its our privilege.

And if this IS love, I hope you're the one,
But every encounter is different.
Between long and short runs,
Let's just make this one deliberate.

www.ingramcontent.com/pod-product-compliance
Lightning Source LLC
LaVergne TN
LVHW041256200726
843507LV00013B/2993